THE BATTLE FOR YOUR BRAIN

Psychological Warfare

By

Viorel Serb

ISBN: 978-973-0-34154-6

Satu Mare 2021

Disclaimer

This book was written to be informative and educational, the reader, and only the reader is responsible for its actions.

I am not an expert nor am I qualified in any of the fields, all the information presented in this book is based on my personal experience and my intense research.

NOTE:

The YouTube links were put in for the ebook version.

I have decided to leave the YouTube links included in this version of the book too.

Clickable links inside the PDF file.

Free PDF version of this book included.
Scan the QR code on the back of this book to read/download it in PDF.

Tip:

Take advantage of the empty spaces left in this book and add your notes/ ideas that pop up in your head while reading this book.

Scan the QR code to download a free Flyer

With all this being said, please proceed further ;)

About Me

I've been a Targeted Individual for approximately 10 years.
This "program" made me lose everything I had, family, friends, girlfriends, my home, university, jobs, money, business plans, business opportunities, my once very good health, pretty much everything.

At first, I took it as a joke, then it became confusing, then it was overwhelming and got more intense. I got covertly, poisoned, and drugged, they tried to destroy the most valuable thing that I had and still have, which is my brain.

Few years passed by and I didn't know what was happening to me, until one day, I've come across a Youtube Video called:
The Gangstalking Program Explained

After watching this video, everything started to connect and make sense.

I thought this is temporary, and it will eventually

stop. I didn't put too much effort into stopping it, mainly because I knew the people who were harassing me, so it didn't seem too dangerous until they tried to kill me few times.

As years passed by, I've done more and more research into the Gang Stalking topic, I've realized that this is a "slow kill program" and it only ends when the victim is dead.

Last year (2020) I've decided to put an end to this "slow kill program", for me and every victim. After thousands of hours of reading and research, I've concluded that to stop this, we the Targeted Individuals, need to educate ourselves and educate the general public.

If the general public refuses to participate, this will be Game Over.

Let's unite, expose, and fight to stop Gang Stalking.

TABLE OF CONTENTS

Chapter 5

TACTICS AND TECHNIQUES...-32

Chapter 6

OTHER TACTICS AND TECHNIQUES...-82

Chapter 7

FACTS THAT CAN'T BE DENIED...-85

Chapter 8

RESOURCES FOR TARGETED INDIVIDUALS...-97

Introduction

What is Gang Stalking ?!?

It's a "slow kill program" - A Combination of Cointelpro and Mk-Ultra, both black ops government programs.
It has its roots in The East German Stasi Zerzetzung "Decomposition"

This "slow kill program" is a form of community mobbing and organized stalking combined.
Just like you have workplace mobbing, and online mobbing, which are both fully recognized as legitimate, this is also the community form, plus electronic harassment.

In summary: The constant struggle of the dumb people to rule over the smart people.

What is a Targeted Individual (TI) ?!?

A person who has become targeted by any party, organization or entity. A person can become targeted from entities ranging from corruption in business, organized crime, cults & extremists or by government. A person who becomes targeted will face campaigns of surveillance of different degrees and generally speaking campaigns that negatively impact an individual. This could range from campaigns to harass, discredit, sabotage, instill fear and paranoia, manipulate, extort, or even assassinate; among others.

John blew the whistle on wrong doing within the company he worked for and became a targeted individual.

by thatradtallguy June 10, 2016

Source:
https://www.urbandictionary.com/define.php?term=targeted%20individual

Types of Targeted Individuals

Targeted by the Government

According to former DOD employee Bryan Tew, who became a targeted individual himself, there are four categories of targeted individuals:

1. Judicial Targets
- Those who have committed a crime or those who are suspected they have committed a crime

2. Extra-Judicial Targets
- This category range from Those Suspected they might have committed a crime but there is no evidence, all the way to Activists, Whistleblowers ...etc

3. Target of opportunity
- That's a very large area, everybody can fall in there.
- People who are randomly targeted for science, human experimentation, for the purpose of research and development

4. Lucrative targets
- People who have access to/or might possess sensitive information or who might have access to sensitive positions

Targeted by Non Government Groups or Former Gov. Peersonnel

This former gov personnel has access to government classified technology, and the clearance to do it. Often these individuals advertise their services on the internet as:
- Private investigator for hire
- Life ruining services for hire
- Reputation damage for hire
- Revenge for hire
- Murder for hire
- Monitoring a cheating spouse
- Corporate espionage

Anyone can become targeted by these types of people for countless reasons. Few examples:
- A bad break up
- Fights between children
- Disagreements between neighbors
- Envious co-workers
- Envious friends or acquaintances, relatives
- Fight over a lover
- Eliminating competition
- Work competition
- Friend turned enemy
- Bad divorce
- Basically, anyone can become a targeted individual for any reason.

Targeted By Hackers

Hackers who have copied and re-created, or stole the mind control technology, use it against people, and pretend to be the government.

This type of Targeting is based on financial gains for the hackers.

These types of Ti's are mostly victims of:
Theft
- Cash
- Expensive objects (Guns, Coins, Collectibles, Gold...etc)
- Fraudulent bank transfers(stealing the Tis money)
- Intellectual property theft
- Identity Theft
- Hackers take Life insurance for Ti's and then drive the Ti's to suicide to collect the insurance money

Voyeurism
Voyeurism is the sexual interest in or practice of watching other people engaged in intimate behaviors, such as undressing, sexual activity, or other actions usually considered to be of a private nature
Source: https://en.wikipedia.org/wiki/Voyeurism

- Ti's life is live-streamed online, perps charge,

a fee, anyone can watch the live streams, these websites are shared among criminal organizations.

Snuff films / videos
A snuff film, or snuff movie, is "a movie in a purported genre of movies in which a person is actually murdered or commits suicide. It may or may not be made for financial gain, but is supposedly 'circulated amongst a jaded few for the purpose of entertainment'"
Source: https://en.wikipedia.org/wiki/Snuff_film

- Ti's life is live-streamed online, perps charge, a fee, anyone can watch the live streams, these websites are shared among criminal organizations.

Note - IMPORTANT - No matter whom the ti is targeted by, the tactics, techniques, and technology used are identical.
That's what makes it hard for ti's to identify who's targetting them.

These Hackers will use Hats, T-shirts, and other objects embedded with the FBI's or CIA's logo.
Sometimes even changing the name of the nearby wifi's into something like CIA Van, FBI Surveillance, D.O.D team...etc

Recommended Videos

Types of Targeted Individuals - Gang Stalking - Cyber Torture - Electronic Harassment

Gang stalking : Conversation Between A Perp And A Target from Bright Light On Black Shadows 2015

Gang Stalking - Targeted Individuals - Dark Web Wireless Prison - Cyber Torture

There are 6 outcomes for Targeted Individuals
- Ti's end up locked up into mental institutions
- Ti's commit Suicide
- Ti's lose their mind and go on a killing spree
- Ti's end up broke, homeless, and helpless
- Ti's end up drug addicts
- Ti's expose the Program and take their lives back

Electronic Harassment

Voice to Skull(V2K) - Synthetic Telepathy

V2K - voice to skull device - is a weapon use for transmitting voices with low or high frequencies. Voices can be for commands or harassments attacks that may look like the TI's own voice. V2K can also use to induce or manipulate dreams or to deprived TI sleeps.

One especially invasive attack method in the arena of 'psycho-electronic' mind control is 'voice to skull'. Voice to skull is the transmission of voice, or any other audible or subliminal sound, directly into the hearing sense of the mind control victim.

It is common for psycho-electronic mind control victims to report a very frequent or constant "ringing in the ears", which is also a symptom of the "Lowery" method of subliminal voice conversion. Lowery's method is described in U.S. patent 5,159,703 and such a converter can easily be built by someone with reasonable electronic assembly abilities. **Source: the7thfire.com**

In actual fact, a suitably modified amateur radio transmitter operating in either the 420 to 450 megahertz band or the 1.3 gigahertz band, with a highly directional antenna, is capable of transmitting voice to skull signals at less cost than the price of an automobile.

Source:
https://sites.google.com/site/targetedindividuals101/home/v2k

Recommended Videos
Gang Stalking - Voice to skull - Synthetic Telepathy - Targeted Individuals - Cyber Torture

Detecting Incoming Sound - Voice to skull (V2K)
Dr. Rauni Kilde explains how - Min 06:55
Schizophrenia Or Not

Remote Neural Monitoring - RNM

Remote Neural Monitoring is a form of functional neuroimaging, claimed to have been developed by the National Security Agency(NSA), that is capable of extracting EEG data from the human brain at a distance with no contacts or electrodes required.

It is further claimed that the NSA has the capablility to decode this data to extract subvocalizations, visual and auditory data.
In effect it allows access to a person's thoughts without their knowledge or permission.

It has been alleged that various organizations have been using Remote Neural Monitoring on US and other citizens for surveillance and harassment purposes.
Source: http://www.greatdreams.com/RNM.htm

Recommenden Videos

Gang Stalking : DEW, Sonic, Low Frequency Weapons - Mind Control Behavior control - PATENTS REVIEW

Gang Stalking Technology - Everything YOU NEED TO KNOW !?!

Dream manipulation

Dream management, dream manipulation, or induced dreams is done to reprogram the target's subconscious mind.

How to identify an induced dream !?!
I will explain it based on personal experience. We all watch movies and videos, and we all remember them clearly for the next few days, the same can be said about induced dreams.

You will remember the dream as if you were watching a movie, a movie in which you are the "actor" and the "spectator" at the same time, the most frightening part is that you do not have control over what you say or do.

When and if you do know yourself and realize that something is going on and that the reaction or sentence is not something you would say or do, and you try to take control over "your body"(mind), you will wake up.

That's one way how you can identify an induced dream.

Note:
If you mention induced dreams to anyone, you might end up being diagnosed as suffering from PTSD(post-traumatic stress disorder. Gang stalkers have a mental disorder on the psychiatry book for many of their tactics and techniques.

There isn't any specific method that you can use to gather evidence on this. (I couldn't find any method, if anyone knows how to, let us all know)

The same method used to record V2K might work to record induced dreams. (This is just my theory, it might or might not work)

Induced Paranoia

Every Ti has its inner voice read (mind-reading - RNM), what the technology can do, is to clone your inner voice, beam it back to you via voice to skull (V2K) and make you believe that it is your inner voice /thoughts, and make you think that the idea/thought is your own.
Very dangerous stuff.

One example would be:
The Gangstalkers will implant a visual or audio memory in your brain.
The visual or audio memory can be implanted in your brain via social media, a conversation you had with someone, a "stranger" passing by saying certain things...etc.

They will make up scenarios and beam them scenarios into your brain via voice to skull(V2K) as if it is your inner voice.

They might add fear and panic frequencies to the V2K, to make you feel agitated, panicked, confused...etc
If you feel agitated, panicked, and confused, and you cannot control your mind, you are being mind-controlled.
It's time to get your measuring devices and start getting some evidence.

Forced Speech

Explanation by Dr. Robert Duncan

"So the way you experience it be, I, I guess like Tourette's , almost like, uh you can't control what is coming out of your mouth, and uh it's not what's in your thought processes but you're speaking somebody else's verbiage, and uh, and yes, it does take a long time for that usually to occur, because remember, your brain has been mapped out, and uh, so they uh mapped out your audio cortex, you're cloned with another person or a machine, and so pretty soon the brain will uh bypass your cerebral cortex and be able to shoot out vocabulary that you have no intention of saying, and it's, I hate to say it but it's pretty common with most iT's."

Recommended Video

Watch the video below, at min. 14:52 to listen to Dr. Robert Duncan's explanation on how forced speech is done:

Gang Stalking Technology - Everything YOU NEED TO KNOW !?!

Note:

Gangstalkers use this tactic when the Ti's meet new people and are having important conversations.
For example:
- The Ti is going on a date.
- The Ti is meeting a potential business partner, client, has a job interview, etc.
- The Ti is having a serious conversation about an important topic.

This tactic is used to make the Ti's look dumb, crazy, say incriminating things, and make Ti's look mentally unstable.
These tactics are also used on Ti's relatives.
It is used to make them say things that they wouldn't say, such as trigger words for Ti.

Let's Discuss Frequencies
National Security Agency Signals Intelligence Electronic Brain Link Technology

NSA SigInt can remotely detect, identify and monitor a person's bioelectric fields. The NSA's Signals Intelligence has the proprietary ability to remotely and non-invasively monitor information in the human brain by digitally decoding the evoked potentials in the 30-50 hz, .5 milliwatt electro-magnetic emissions from the brain. Neuronal activity in the brain creates a shifting electrical pattern that has a shifting magnetic flux. This magnetic flux puts out a constant 30-50 hz, .5 milliwatt electromagnetic (EMF) wave. Contained in the electromagnetic emis- sion from the brain are spikes and patterns called "evoked potentials." Every thought, reaction, motor command, auditory event, and visual image in the brain has a corresponding "evoked potential" or set of "evoked potentials." The EMF emission from the brain can be decoded into the current thoughts, images and sounds in the subject's brain. NSA SigInt uses **EMF-transmitted Brain Stimulation** as a communications system to transmit information (as well as nervous system messages) to intelligence agents and also to transmit to the brains of covert operations sub- jects (on a non-perceptible level). **EMF Brain Stimulation** works by sending a complexly coded and pulsed electromagnetic signal to trigger evoked potentials (events) in the brain, thereby forming sound and visual images in the brain's neural circuits. EMF Brain Stimulation can also change a person's brain-states and affect motor control. **Two-way Electronic Brain-Link** is done by remotely monitoring neural audio-visual information while transmit- ting sound to the auditory cortex (bypassing the ears) and transmitting faint images to the visual cortex (bypassing the optic nerves and eyes, the images appear as floating 2-D screens in the brain).

Two-Way Electronic Brain Link has become the ultimate communications system for CIA/NSA personnel. Remo- te Neural Monitoring (RNM, remotely monitoring bioelectric information in the human brain) has become the ulti- mate surveillance system. It is used by a limited number of agents in the U.S. Intelligence Community. RNM requires decoding the resonance frequency of each specific brain area. That frequency is then modulated in order to impose information in That specific brain area. The frequency to which the various brain areas respond varies from 3 Hz to 50 Hz. Only NSA Signals Intelligence modulates signals in this frequency band.
An example of EMF Brain Stimulation:

Brain Area	Bioelectric Resonance Frequency	Information Induced Through Modulation
Motor Control Cortex	10 HZ	Motor Impulse Co-ordination
Auditory Cortex	15 HZ	Sound which bypasses the ears
Visual Cortex	25 HZ	Images in the brain, bypassing the eyes
Somatosensory Cortex	09 HZ	Phantom Touch Sense
Thought Center	20 HZ	Imposed Subconscious Thoughts

This modulated information can be put into the brain at varying intensities from subliminal to perceptible. Each person's brain has a unique set of bioelectric resonance/entrainment frequencies. Sending audio information to a person's brain at the frequency of another person's auditory cortex would result in that audio information not being perceived. The Plaintiff learned of RNM by being in two-way RNM contact with the Kinnecome group at the NSA, Ft. Meade. They used RNM 3D sound direct to the brain to harass the Plaintiff from 10/90 to 5/91. As of 5/91 they have had two-way RNM communications with the Plaintiff and have used RNM to attempt to incapacitate the Plaintiff and hinder the Plaintiff from going to authorities about their activities against the Plaintiff in the last twelve years. The Kinnecome group has about 100 persons working 24-hours-a-day at Ft Meade. They have also brain-tapped persons the Plaintiff is in contact with to keep the Plaintiff isolated. This is the first time ever that a private citizen has been harassed with RNM and has been able to bring a lawsuit against NSA personnel misusing this intelligence operations method.

Source: **John St. Clair Akwei vs. NSA, Ft. Meade, MD, USA**

Note: Only NSA Signal Intelligence modulates Signals in this Frequency Band
Acording to the document from the court case Akwei vs NSA, NSA is using mind control frequencies ranging from 3Hz to 50 Hz.

Decting ELF(Extremely Low Frequency)

There is something called ELF(Extremely Low Frequency) Meter, with a bandwidth range from 5Hz to 3500MHz
When looking to buy an ELF meter, make sure that it is bandwidth is between 5Hz to 3500MHz.

Spectrum analyzer

Hand-held spectrum analyzer which can be connected to a computer and the readings analyzed with specific software.
The bandwidth of these analyzers can start at 1 Hz to 30 MHz.

Detecting Incoming Sound - Voice to skull (V2K)

Dr. Rauni Kilde explains how - Min 06:55
Schizophrenia Or Not

Acording to **Dr. Rauni Kilde,**
Voice to Skull(V2K) can be detected with a sensitive microphone called The blue mouse. The most sensitive Blue mouse microphone has a Frequency response of **20Hz-20kHz**, which is similar to the **Human Audio Spectrum.**
There are very few sensitive microphones with a Frequency response of **10Hz to 20kHz,** but there are, you can find them.

According to the document presented above, *"15Hz Sounds which bypasses the ears"*, if the numbers are correct, then Dr. Rauni Kilde was right, the incoming V2K can be detected with a sensitive microphone.

Other Tools Used To Detect ELF/EMF/RF/Microwave...etc

- Oscilloscope and Spectrum Analyzers
- RF spectrum analyzers / software
- TriField® Meter Model 100XE
- Tone generator analyser
- Arduino sound level meter and spectrum analyzer
- Acousticom 2 EMF Meter
- Android App: advance spectrum analizer pro
- Audacity - free audio software
- Aaronia AG - EMC spectrum analyzer SPECTRAN NF Handheld
1Hz - 30MHz | 1pT bis 500µT

Watch the video below to hear a short explanation of the equipment used to prove Electronic Harassment in court.

Gangstalking : Targeted Individual - Kathleen Watterson - Court Case - Short Summary

Detecting Microchips / Implants

International Center Against Abuse of Covert Technologies (ICAACT)
Scannig of Magnus Olsson and other Targeted Individuals.

Gang Stalking - Scanning of Mr. Magnus Olsson and other Targeted Individuals - Cyber Torture

Equipment used to detect brain and body implants:
- Aceco **FC6002MK** radio frequency tracer
- Aceco **FC1001** hand-held frequency counter

Burning Small Implants

Recommended Video

Gang Stalking - How to Burn Body Implants - EMP Gun - EMP Shield Fabric - Targeted Individuals

Lockheed Martin GPS Satellite tracking is done at **3600 - 3750 MHz**. The Vircator microwave weapon (**Patent 4345220**) operates at **3920 - 3935 MHz**. Reading taken in the summer of 2016 with **Spectran HF-4040**. **Caution:** the NSA can hack the device within minutes and "zero out" large sections of the bandwidth. A signal analyzer should be used in combination with a signal generator to prove the readings.

"Dr. Ross Adey has found out that by using **0.75 milliwatts per square centimeter** intensity of pulse **modulated microwaves**, at a frequency of **450 MHz**, it is possible to control ALL aspects of human behavior!" - **Dr. Rauni Leena Kilde, MD**
Source : https://www.targetedjustice.com/

Detecting RF on a Phone Spectrum analizer

I was using an android app called: **Advanced Spectrum Analyzer Pro.**
I've got similar readings with another TI, called *Valerie Ann.*
We used different apps, and we live in different countries.
She shared her **spectrum analyzer** readings in my Facebook group.
The readings I've got are between 18kHz and 20 kHz, her readings are between 19.1 kHz and 22 kHz.
Pretty much identical, considering we both use our cell phone to detect the incoming frequencies, and the accuracy of the phone is not 100%

Acoustic emitters used as a weapon strike with ultrasonic radiation - a wavelength of about 0.017 m, frequencies above 20kHz.

Weapons that strike with ultrasonic radiation (can work from various power sources, both from a 220 volt network and from a battery for a long time) can be used by criminals for general or local human exposure.

The general method of influence is used for initial suppression, depression of body's immune system, deterioration of well-being, bringing the object into a passive state with complete suppression of any resistance, etc.

The principle of operation is ultrasonic pressure.
In other words, the effect on the human psyche of acoustic oscillations of ultra-high frequency. The product acts according to a random law of changing the frequency of a signal a- modulate signal. The so-called bio-noise method.

Every second, a flurry of new frequencies falls upon a person, possibly causing either furious rage, sometimes gloomy apathy, now intense pain, now uncontrollable fun, now wild horror.

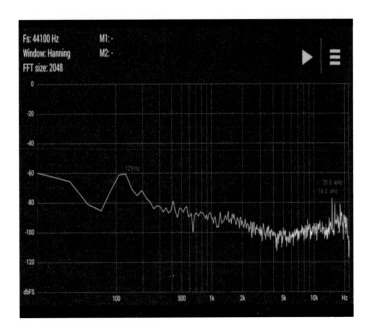

Fs: 44100 Hz   M1: -
Window: Hanning   M2: -
FFT size: 2048

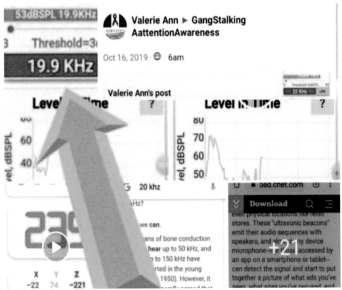

State inducing frequencies

- 40-80 Hz - Alters mood, emotion, sleep states
- 1-8hz Method and Device for Producing a Desired Brain State via magnetic waves
- 100, 110, 210 MHz Anpc.paratus and method for remotely monitoring and altering a target's brain waves / central nervous system
- 1/2 - 2.5 Hz Induces desired emotional state through remote EMFs. E.g sleepiness, sexual arousal

1.8 Hz - Deep Delta sleep
2.5 Hz - Disorientation / tires
4.5 Hz - Paranoia
6.28Hz - Depression
8   Hz - Animal fall asleep
10 Hz - Hypnotic / Calming
10.83Hz - Anger/ outbusrst
10.83Hz - Anger/ outbusrst
11 Hz - Anger
11-13 Hz - Sleep depravation
25 Hz - Blindness / Heart Attack

Disclaimer: The Frequencies above were collected from various sources, some of them might not be accurate, please do more research.

I will just leave this here :

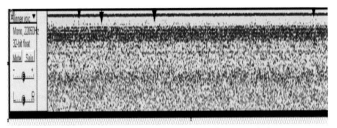

This is a pitch (EAC) analysis of the white noise of a scanner during a severe voice to skull attack on a victim. Disclaimer: It is illegal to modify scanners to view military frequencies. All scanners are disabled in certain frequency ranges for "National Security" reasons. So we used body resonance frequencies just above the military bands when collecting our data. OK? God forbid that people have a right to defend themselves to see what energy frequencies are being used to attack and kill them.

Source: THE MATRIX Deciphered
Psychic Warfare – The Top Secret Mind
Interfacing Technology
Decrypted by *The Saint*

Tactics and Techniques

PO- PsyOp- Psychological Operations–

US Military states that the ultimate goal of PO is to modify the behavior of the TA (TI) by destroying their will.

This is brought about by continually inflicting pain. This is accomplished by a relentless campaign used to demoralize the TI that will create perpetual feelings of intense fear and hopelessness.

The DOD describes this as an "attrition-based approach:" "Attrition is the product or gradual erosion of the will. The victim of this psychological attrition gradually becomes convinced that nothing he can do will yield a satisfactory outcome to a situation."

In PO, themes are used to transmit painful stimuli (also called triggers) through all his/her channels of communication which a TA (TI) has been sensitized to.

Triggers/themes are understood at the strategic, operational, and tactical levels of the campaign and they are passed to various commanders of particular AO if the TA moves towards that portion of the battlespace.

*The triggers **are part of a** behavior modification program called NLP (neuro-linguistic programming) **which uses** anchors and triggers **to promote change.***

An anchor **is created when an emotional state is linked to something such as an object, person, sound, smell, place, color, etc.**

Once the anchor **is established, whatever the individual was exposed to during the** anchoring **process becomes the stimulus (**trigger**) that will provoke the emotion.**

So basically, PO is simply a series of "stimulus-response" interactions.

PO- PsyOp- Psychological Operations - **Source: Bright Lights on Dark Shadows - By Dr. Rauni Kilde**

Drugging & Poisoning

Chemicals and Drugs into Residential Buildings with hidden NSA-Installed and maintained plastic plumbing lines.

a) The NSA has kits for running lines into residential tap water and air ducts of subjects for the delivery of drugs (such as sleeping gas or brainwashing aiding drugs). This is an outgrowth of CIA pharmapsychology.
Source: **John St. Clair Akwei vs. NSA, Ft. Meade, MD, USA, document.**

I was covertly drugged. When I took a drug test I've discovered that I had the following drugs in my system.
- Opiates
- Benzphetamine
- Cocaine
I wasn't on any medication or done any drugs at the time.
Other Ti's were complaining about being covertly drugged.
Some Ti's said that they had the following drugs in their system:
- Phencyclidine (PCP)
- Amphetamine
- Methamphetamine (mAMP)
- Amphetamine (AMP)
- Methadone (MTD)

Anyone can buy urine drug test kits, and do a drug test at home, even keep one with them, and do a drug test anywhere.

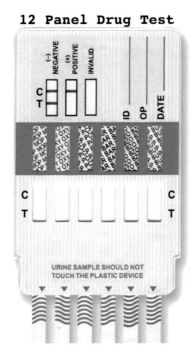

Mobbing

Mobbing, as a sociological term, means bullying of an individual by a group, in any context, such as a family, peer group, school, workplace, neighborhood, community, or online.

When it occurs as physical and emotional abuse in the workplace, such as "ganging up" by co-workers, subordinates or superiors, to force someone out of the workplace through rumor, innuendo, intimidation, humiliation, discrediting, and isolation, it is also referred to as malicious, nonsexual, non-racial/racial, general harassment.

Source: https://en.wikipedia.org/wiki/Mobbing

Gaslighting

Gaslighting is a form of psychological manipulation in which a person or a group covertly sows seeds of doubt in a targeted individual or group, making them question their memory, perception, or judgment.

It may evoke changes in them such as cognitive dissonance or low self-esteem, rendering the victim additionally dependent on the gaslighter for emotional support and validation.

Using denial, misdirection, contradiction, and misinformation, gaslighting involves attempts to destabilize the victim and delegitimize the victim's beliefs.

Mimicking

Definition:
To copy, to imitate, in action, speech, expression, gesture...etc
To copy to mock, ridicule, bully.

Gang Stalkers copy and imitate what Ti does.
Examples:
- Dress in similar color clothing
- Buy the same products in the supermarket
- Leave home at the same time as the Ti
- Repeating the same expressions the Ti is using
- Copying pretty much everything that the Ti is doing
- Takes out the garbage at the same time

It's a psychological form of harassment, to let the Ti know that he/she is under constant surveillance. This tactic is used to intimidate the Ti.

Hand Gestures

This tactic is designed to keep the Ti under a constant state of fear and stress.

If the Ti is walking to the supermarket, on the way to the supermarket and back, also inside the supermarket, the Ti will see a large number of people touching the same part of their bodies, for example:
- Nose touching
- One eye covering
- Belly touching
- Touching the head
- Touching the ear
- Showing fists
- Horn sign
- Clapping
- Cover the mouth

You might say that people touch their body parts all the time, and it is just a coincidence, but the large number of people touching the same parts of their bodies in a very short period is less likely to be a coincidence.

Noise Harassment Campaigns

The noise campaigns can also include and not limited to :
- Neighbours playing loud music when the Ti is trying to sleep
- Landscaping work when the Ti is trying to sleep
- Neighbours using building equipment early in the morning or at specific times when the Ti is trying to sleep
- Kids playing with the ball and kick it in the walls of Ti's home
- Kids shouting
- Adults shouting
- Cars passing by revving the engines
- Doors Slamming
- Loud Coughing
- First responders(police, ambulance, firefighters) passing by with the sirens on ...etc

Other Forms of Noise Harassment
- Coughing
- Clearing Through
- Sneezing
- Fake laughing
- Hitting objects with their hands or feet
- Multiple perps playing the same song on their phone

Recommended Video
Gang stalking : ABC News Couple Harassed with Organized Gang Stalking Noise Harassment Campaign

Sleep Deprivation

Sleep deprivation usually goes hand in hand with noise campaigns.
Gangstalkers might also beam certain frequencies at the Ti's house to keep the Ti awake. These frequencies are between 11 - 13 Hz.

This is done to prevent the Ti to function at its full capacity.
We all know that our brains and bodies do not function well when we are tired and didn't have a good night's sleep.

Advice for Ti's - When Gangstalkers don't let you sleep, do this:
Think of ways how to rationally explain Gangstalking.
Think of ways how to expose Gangstalking.
Think of ways to stop Gangstalking.
Think back in time, try to remember when exactly your life started to fall apart, identify the people who were in your life at the time.
There's always someone envious, jealous, or in competition with you, that's the person who put on the "slow kill program".

Car Accidents - Vandalism

- Sliced tires
- Entering a vehicle cuts to the car's upholstery
- Screenwash liquid replaced with water to cause freezing in winter
- unlocking the car doors and leave them unlocked
- braking off the rear mirror
- scratching the dashboard
- placing small objects in the car
- taking(stealing) small objects from the car
- scratching the car's paint...etc

All this is designed to make the Ti look irresponsible and make him/her look bad if he/she talks to anyone about it.

House Brake-ins - Vandalism

- Ti experiences brake-ins and finds that the furniture has been moved or damaged, certain objects have been rearranged, small objects are gone missing, clothes have been damaged, food has been tampered with, etc

Note: There are small spy cameras that have movement detection, what that means is the camera starts recording when it detects movements.

Also, there is a free app called Alfred Camera, all you need is an old phone and internet connection, either a sim card or your home network.

Street Theater

Street theater is any premeditated harassment that takes place in a public setting, ranging from the dumbfoundingly stupid and simple to the elaborate/sophisticated plan that definitely was not worth it.

– Leaving dead/dying animals in target's path. Squirrels, rats, mice, birds, dogs. Leaving small feathers in targets path repeatedly.

– Saying first or last names of family members/ close friends aloud in public within earshot. Strangers saying target's name in public.

– Crowding stores/shops after you arrive, causing delays in checkout lanes. Preoccupying employees with stupid questions/ requests. Paying for items with copious amounts of change.

– Having cats/ dogs/ children suddenly run into road as you drive by.

– Couples fighting in public w/ loud, abusive language. Younger males cursing, spitting, using vulgar language.
-People talking about severe abuse, suicides, drug abuse in front of target. People pretending to smoke hard drugs in front of target. People

breaking down and crying/sobbing in front of target.

– Same time entry/exit by neighbors. Neighbors showing up at grocery store, pharmacy, cafes, gas station, drive thrus, church, etc.

– Insulting comments about body/hairstyle/appearance/social skills/intelligence level, often said aloud in front of a group in public.

– Completely ignored by retail staff when you need help; then followed around by staff like a rash on your ass when you just want to shop in peace.

– Using artificial telepathy to block items target plans to buy at the store. You can go to the market at 2am and there be a perp blocking the item you want to buy.

– Using directed conversation to humiliate target in public.

Experiencing the types of harassment mentioned above on a daily basis for years can and will lead to PTSD, nervous breakdowns, complete loss of trust in people, severe anxiety, depression, and suicidal/homicidal thoughts. Once the perps have accomplished complete dehumanization and destruction of the target, the target is blamed for all "of their own problems" and the perps walk away scot free.

Read the full article , click the link below
Source: Some Random Street Theater -
https://stoporgangstalking.com/2013/12/10/some-random-street-theater/

Sabotaging the target's reputation

Sabotaging the target's reputation- and all that goes with it, such as ability to earn a living, business and personal relationships- is a very special operations category. Newer community-based agents will not be assigned to "engineer" the method, but will assist in passing "rumours," which are the main means of destroying a target's public image.

"Rumours" consist mainly of lies. However, in order to secure cooperation of specific members of the community to participate in the punishment phase, additional information keyed to appeal to the patriotic or community service sense of such community members may be used as well. As mentioned earlier, the organization has many top psychologists and psychiatrists on permanent staff at headquarters, and some in larger population centers. It is their responsibility to design the campaign to destroy the target's reputation.

These people listed below can be approached and given information which will cause them to make the target's association with them uncomfortable, or break off all contact with the target.

-Business contacts.

-Supervisors.

-Co-workers.

-Casual social contacts, such as clubs a target may be a member of, or a group that frequents a bar where the target is a patron.

-Friends.

-Local fraternal organizations- they are motivated by the public service, and are an excellent source of assistance in keeping the target under surveillance, and participating in the punishment phase as well.

-Store staffs at places the target shops.

-Target's landlord.

-Target's neighbors.

-Tradesmen who are likely to service the target's home, car, or business. -Bus drivers on the target's route. -Local children.

-City employees, including emergency medical technicians, ambulances. -Homeless shelter staff and residents where applicable.

-Family members (surprisingly, many are ready to believe negative information.)

-Especially, personnel at places the target applies for work.

SABOTAGING THE TARGET'S REPUTATION - Source: Bright Lights on Dark Shadows - By Dr. Rauni Kilde

Ruining Relationships - Isolation

Loneliness can be damaging to both our mental and physical health. Socially isolated people are less able to deal with stressful situations. They're also more likely to feel depressed and may have problems processing information. This in turn can lead to difficulties with decision-making and memory storage and recall.

People who are lonely are also more susceptible to illness. Researchers found that a lonely person's immune system responds differently to fighting viruses, making them more likely to develop an illness.

Source: https://www.sciencealert.com/isolation-has-profound-effects-on-the-human-body-and-brain-here-s-what-happens

To accomplish Ti's complete isolation the Gangstalkers are using a combination of the following methods:
- Gaslighting
- Character assassination
- Flying monkeys
- Slander campaigns
- Lies
- Gangstalkers are presenting fake evidence such as pictures, videos, documents, social media accounts, texts, emails, phone calls.

Anyone who might be able to help the Ti is recruited by the Gangstalkers to sabotage and harass the Ti.

Most Ti's struggle with trust issues and refuse to get help from family, friends, acquaintances, doctors, lawyers, or anyone who might be able to help them.

Ti's will eventually isolate themselves, this is a survival mechanism.
This is one of the toughest forms of psychological torture, too many Ti's commit suicides when they have nobody to talk to and when nobody believes and understands them.

Recommended Video
Sometimes the person calling you is not who you think it is.
Use a call recording app.
Gang Stalkers called me and pretended to be my father, my brother ...etc

GangStalking: Phone Spoofing and Voice Transformation /cloning - Targeted Individuals -CyberTorture

Illegal Surveillance

This involves setting up audio and visual surveillance equipment in the Ti's, home, workplace, car.

Examples Of Illegal Surveillance Equipment
- Spy cameras
- Microphones
- Gps trackers
- Phone hacking

There are some bug detectors Ti's can use to detect hidden cameras, hidden microphones, or even to scan their mobile device.

There are multiple types of RF Detectors, cheap and more expensive, some even come with incorporated spycam detectors.

Disclaimer: I am not promoting any brand or any specific products.
You should do your research and buy what you think is best for you.
The products presented below are just a point of reference.

Examples of Bug Detectors
1. This example is the cheap option.
I used one similar and I've got some good results.
See: Rf phone scanning Pic.1 and Pic. 2

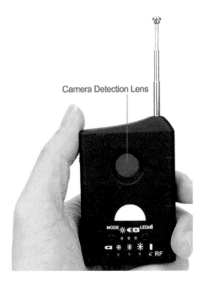

Camera Detection Lens

2. Few more examples

Scanning for hidden spycameras and microphones
How to use one of these devices
Before scanning:
-Turn off wifi routers
-Cordless phones
-Cell phones
-Bluetooth devices
-Turn lights off when scanning for spy cameras

Scanning your mobile device

Your mobile device should not transmit any signal when idle.

If it does, congratulations, your phone is hacked, someone is spying on you.

For more information on how to use a bug detector, ask Google "how to use a bug detector", read articles on various websites, and watch Youtube videos.

Example 1 : Phone is Iddle

Notice the bottom lights of the RF detector are off, no RF detected, meaning no calls, texts, or other connections at that particular moment.

RF Phone Scanning Pic.1

Example 2: Someone is remotelly listening in to your conversation via your phone's microphone

When there is a connection on the phone, the RF detector is picking up the incoming or outgoing connections. The incoming or outgoing connection can be a phone call, text message or someone is remotely activating the microphone or the camera of your device.

Notice the phone in the picture has the screen off, and the rf detector is picking on a signal. That's the exact result you will get if your phone is hacked and someone is listening to your conversations.

Tip: use the RF detector to scan your phone when you are having a conversation with someone, wherever you are in the same room or a different room with the phone. The chances for the microphone to be activated and for someone to listen to you when you are alone are pretty low.

RF Phone sScanning Pic.2

How to stop eavesdroppers

There is something called a "white noise generator" it is used to stop eavesdroppers. If you want to have a very confidential conversation, you might want to check out these little devices.

There are YouTube videos that claim to be white noise.

The white noise can also be bought on a CD or DVD and played, on a laptop, pc, or DVD player.

Device Hacking

Phone / laptop / tablet (spyware, malware)
- Gang stalkers are deleting evidence
- Sabotaging social media accounts
- Sabotaging relationships by making calls, sending text messages, emails...etc
- Bank account transfers
- Deleting pictures and important documents...etc

Signs that your phone is hacked
- Phone battery dries out too quick
- High Data usage
- Phone is slower or freezes
- Phone gets hot, even when you are not using it
- Suspicious activity to any accounts linked to the phone, ex: social media apps, email, WhatsApp ...etc
- New apps installed on your device, apps that you didn't install yourself
- Phone bill higher than usual

Spoofed Phone Calls
Gangstalkers use call spoofing(cloning) and voice transformation/cloning to call the Ti's and pretend to be their family members or friends. This is done to ruin Ti's relationships.

There are free and paid call recording apps, use one.
Keep multiple copies (online and offline)of the suspicious call recordings.
There is audio decoding software that can decode suspicious call recordings.

Recommended Video
GangStalking: Phone Spoofing and Voice Transformation /cloning - Targeted Individuals -CyberTorture

SMS

Gang stalkers will send you various types of messages:
- to harass
- to intimidate
- to threaten you
- to hack your phone, them messages will contain links

Keep multiple copies (screenshots) of the suspicious messages.

E-Mail

Gang stalkers will send you various types of e-mails:
- to harass
- to intimidate
- to scare you
- to hack your phone, computer, tablet, some of the emails will contain malicious links or attachments.

Tip: keep multiple copies (screen shoots/print screens) of the suspicious emails.

Do not click any links or open any attachments.

Examples Of Attacks :

PDF Attack

If you receive a PDF file, you can use an antivirus to scan it, although even if you scan it and it shows as clean, the embedded media in the file might still be infected and undetected by the antivirus.

Another safe alternative might be to open the document in a sandbox.
If you want to be 100% safe, do not open the document if you don't expect one, or it isn't from a trusted source.

recently joined a group called Gang stalking
Aatention awareness by moderator here
same. as iposted some vital information in
regard to this
https://www.ohchr.org/Documents/Issues
/Torture/Call/NGOs/Advforhumankind4.pdf . i
was removed.. its a private group some good
information. this is vital. so i felt my stalker
about and when ever i hit something helful its
removed from me . so they heard my ab... See
More

Write a comment...

Social Media Link's Attack

Similar to PDF files, links can contain malicious software that can infect and hack your device. Do not click any links, especially those links that look like the one's in the picture below.

6GwyTP~& Excellent quality and reasonable price. Lower wholesale price and low-shipping charges. Look for a reliable supplier? Jack is your choice.
If we can be of service, we are at your disposal. Please contact WhatsApp(8615896131671):
http://j2FYN2.linkworka.vip/s/id/61
Citrine DT:Good transparency with shiny rainbows.
Skull: Different kinds of materials.
Green Fluorite sphere: High-quality w... See More

J2FYN2.LINKWORKA.VIP
j2fyn2.linkworka.vip

55m   Like   Reply

Facebook Messenger Video Attack

The video presented below, it's infected with malware.

If you receive one of these videos in Facebook messenger and you click the video, your device will get infected and the attacker will get access to your device

Text Message and Email Attack

There is something called an Email Header, which gives up a lot of pieces of information about your device when you send emails. Email headers show the following information:
- Ip address (can be used to geolocate you, also can be used in man in the middle attacks, and other methods to spy on your network and capture your information)
- Local time and times zones
- System name, hostnames, and internal domain name
- SMTP AUTH user name or client-cert use...etc
- And much more

I've reset the phone to factory settings, that means no more Spyware and malware. Few days latter this:

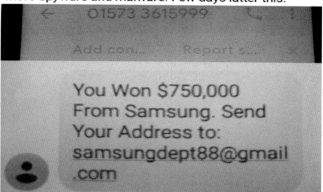

Another form of email attack

In the example presented below, the malicious link is embedded in the button **"Cancel Request"**

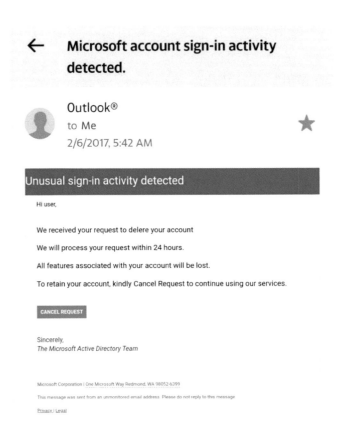

Email Attack Phishing

Phishing is the fraudulent attempt to obtain sensitive information or data, such as usernames, passwords and credit card details or other sensitive details, by impersonating oneself as a trustworthy entity in a digital communication. Typically carried out by email spoofing, instant messaging, and text messaging, phishing often directs users to enter personal information at a fake website which matches the look and feel of the legitimate site.

Text Source:
https://en.wikipedia.org/wiki/Phishing

← **Unexpected sign-in attempt**

Yahoo
to Me
4/21/2016, 6:26 PM

Hi Numele,

On Thu, Apr 21, 2016 5:26 PM GMT+2, we noticed a successful sign in to your Yahoo account **sviog** from an unrecognized device in France.

If this was you, you're all set!

If this wasn't you and believe someone may have tried to access your account, please **change your password** and update your account recovery information.

Yahoo

Replies sent to this email cannot be answered.

Fraudulent Log In into my email

I have found a Draft email, in my email, an email that I haven't used in a while. Someone logged in to my email and was sending emails, pretending to be me.

Draft means that an email is written and not sent, waiting to be sent.

This is a perfect example of why you should activate the 2-factor authentification.

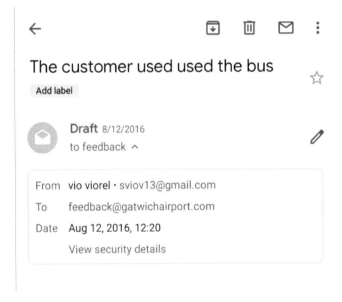

Other ways your device can get hacked

Other forms of malware and spyware can be installed on the device if someone has physical access to the device.
Make sure that you keep your device with you at all times.

Final thoughts

If you have received any of the messages, emails, pictures, or videos presented above, and you clicked on them, congratulations , your device is hacked :)

What can you do ?!?

Phone forensic software can detect any spyware, malware, keyloggers, or other malicious software installed on your phone.

If you can have your phone scanned by phone forensic software, do so.
In this case, you will be able to prove that your phone has been hacked.

If you can't get your phone scanned by forensic software, you can reset your phone to factory settings, make sure that you save any important documents, pictures, contacts, files, before you reset the phone to factory settings.

After you reset your phone to factory

setting you should:
Do
- Change your passwords for emails, social media, websites ...etc
- Use strong passwords: 16 characters or more, capital letters, numbers, and symbols. **Example: Hv6La4@XC4s$NwNz0G!Ha***
- Activate 2-factor authentification
- After activating the 2-factor authentification, log in to your accounts, go to settings, security, and log out on all devices.
- Use a VPN
- Keep apps updated
- Delete any apps you are not using
- Keep your device software updated
- Do your research on how to stay safe online
- Do keep an eye on your phone to check for any signs that your phone has been hacked.

Don't
- Don't click suspicious links in text messages or social media
- Don't use public wifi without a VPN
- Don't open or respond to suspicious e-mails
- Don't click suspicious document files, such as PDF, DOC, TXT, or any other format.
- Don't give your passwords to anyone
- Don't let anyone use your phone

You might be thinking, what's the point to secure my device, they know everything that I do, they hacked my brain!

That might be true, but if you secure your device they won't de able to log in to your accounts and do the following:
- Delete important emails, contacts, messages, documents, pictures
- Send emails or messages pretending to be you
- And much more

Disclamer : I'm not a cyber security expert.
I might have missed some critical informations, but I am giving you the best advice I can, based on my personal experience and research.
The information presented above helped me to keep my devices relatively safe.

Intimidation

- Ti's will be threatened to be killed, or have one or more of their family members killed. This is a direct threat to my life.

Email

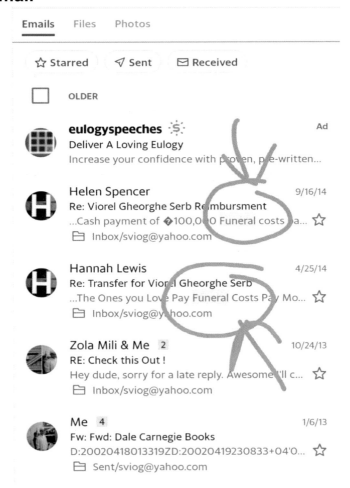

Facebook

THINK ...i
31m

Even if someone got a gun
and shot you in the head, it was
nothing personal

😆 Haha   💬 Comment   ➤ Share

😬 Vio Serb

Vio Serb
I'm so scared, should I just stay inside the
house for the rest of my life?!? 😭😰😬

14m   Like   Reply   1 😬

THINK ___ Vio Serb its your choice .. imma be weir...

Vio Serb ___ bullets can't stop the truth 😊

THINK ___ i there you are

Vio Serb
And just stop everything that I'm doing, that's
what I should do? 🧍

😬😬😬

13m   Like   Reply   1 😬

THINK ___ Vio Serb do whatever u wanna do..but w...

Vio Serb N___ 🖤 love is in the air, love is eve...

Cyber Bullying - Cyber Harassment - Cyber Stalking

Cyberbullying, also referred to legally as cyber harassment, is defined as using the internet (social media, email, etc.), cell phones, or other technology to send text or images intended to hurt or embarrass another person.

Cyberbullying includes sending hurtful words and images, pretending to be another person online, sending hate mail, stalking, and doing other harmful behaviors. When people talk about cyberbullying in general, cyberstalking is not often discussed, but it is also a serious issue.

Alabama Laws on Cyberstalking
Cyberstalking is covered in the general stalking laws of Alabama. Stalking is defined by Alabama law as someone who is repeatedly harassing, threatening, or creating fear in another person by means of physical, verbal, or electronic communication.

Stalking charges are serious and can be designated a felony. Individuals convicted of stalking in Alabama can be fined, assigned a restraining order, receive probation, or be sentenced to 1 to 20 years in prison. In 2011, a 12-year-old girl convicted of cyberstalking was sentenced to 6 months of probation and 20 hours of community service, along with mandatory adult supervision of all computer usage.

Penalties for breaking stalking laws include the following:

- Stalking in the first degree is a Class C felony punishable by a sentence of 1 to 10 years in prison and up to a $15,000
- Stalking in the second degree is a Class B misdemeanor punishable by not more than 6 months in jail and a $3,000
- Aggravated stalking in the first degree is a Class B felony punishable by a sentence of 2 to 20 years in prison and at least a $30,000
- Aggravated stalking in the second degree is a Class C felony punished the same as stalking in the first degree.

Source: https://www.aces.edu/blog/topics/home-family/advancing-bullying-awareness-cyberbullying-cyberstalking-sexting-the-law/?cn-reloaded=1

Recommended Videos

GangStalking, Targeted individuals, Cyber Harassment, Cyber stalking, Cyber Torture, Sensitization

Gang stalking - Cyber Stalking and Harassment - Targeted Individuals - Cyber Torture

Synthetic Reality

You need to understand this :
The triggers are part of a behavior modification program called NLP (neuro-linguistic programming) which uses **anchors and triggers** to promote change. An **anchor** is created when an emotional state is linked to something such as an object, person, sound, smell, place, color, etc. Once the **anchor** is established, whatever the individual was exposed to during the **anchoring** process becomes the stimulus (**trigger**) that will provoke the emotion. So basically, PO is simply a series of "stimulus-response" interactions.

Here are few examples:
- Certain celebrity is stalking the Ti
- The aliens are communicating with the Ti - This is done via Voice to skull
- The spirits are talking to the Ti -This is done via Voice to skull
- The CIA is talking to the Ti and wants the Ti to accomplish a mission
- Certain politician is stealing the Ti's ideas
- The Illuminati is harassing the Ti

Let's take the following scenario:
The Gangstalkers will make the Ti believe that Celine Dion is harassing them. This is How it's done!

It is done using the same methods over and over again, these methods are sensitization-anchoring-*triggers.*

Gangstalkers will create newspaper articles, social media posts, Youtube videos, and other materials which will become the sensitization-anchors.
Those materials will include the name and pictures of Celine Dion.

After a while of seeing the same sensitization-anchors, the Ti will associate any further materials that include the sensitization-anchors as a message for him/her.

The materials are made to appear as if Celin Dion is communicating with the TI.

Other Tactics and Techniques

Colour harassment
- Followed by people wearing the same color clothing
- Followed by same color cars
- Social media posts with the same background color...etc

Car harassment / object harassment
- Followed by same color cars
- Followed by cars that carry the same attachments, as bicycles racks, horse trailers, top storage compartment...etc

Bycicle harssment
- People on bicycles will follow the Ti everywhere and do color harassment or noise campaigns.

Pedestrian harassment
- People on foot will follow the Ti everywhere and do color harassment or noise campaigns.

Number harassment

- People walking by repeating the same numbers
- People walking by and wearing t-shirts embedded with the same number
- At work coworkers repeating the same numbers
- Friends and acquaintances of the Tis repeating the same numbers

Extortion

- Ti's are asked to pay a certain amount of money for the harassment and torture to stop

Death Threats

- On social media
- Email
- Text
- Calls

Rape - Black mail

- Ti might have been raped and filmed, the gang stalkers threaten to make the recording public if the Ti talks about it or doesn't do a certain thing for the gang stalkers.

Intimidation

- Ti will be threatened to be killed, or have one or more members of its family killed

Call Harassment

- Ti is receiving a large number of "wrong number" calls
- Ti receives threatening calls or texts

Facts That Can't Be Denied

Technology - Patents

Hearing Device

A method and apparatus for simulation of hearing in mammals by introduction of a **plurality of microwaves** into the region of the auditory cortex is shown and described. A microphone is used to transform sound signals into electrical signals which are in turn analyzed and processed to provide controls for generating a plurality of microwave signals at different frequencies.
Patent Number: **4,858,612**
Date of Patent: **Aug. 22, 1989**

Hearing System

Sound is induced in the head of a person by **radiating the head with microwaves** in the range of 100 megahertz to 10,000 megahertz that are modulated with a particular waveform.
Patent Number: **4,877,027**
Date of Patent: **Oct. 31, 1989**

Apparatus for audibly communicating speech using the **radio frequency hearing** effect
Patent Number: **US6587729B2**
Date of Patent: **Jul. 1, 2003**

Method & Device for Implementing **Radio Frequency Hearing** Effect
Patent Number: **6,470,214 B1**
Date of Patent: **Oct. 22, 2002**

Apparatus & Method of Broadcasting Audible Sound

Using **Ultrasonic Sound** as a Carrier
Patent Number: **6,052,336**
Date of Patent: **Apr. 18, 2000**

Method and device for producing a desired brain state
Patent Number: **US6488617B1**

Communication system and method including brain
wave analysis and/or use of brain activity
Patent Number: **US6011991A**

Ultrasonic Speech Translator & Communications
System
Patent Number: **5,539,705**
Date of Patent: **Jul. 23, 1996**

Method and an Associated Apparatus for Remotely
Determining Information as to Person's Emotional
State
Patent Number: **5,507,291**
Date of Patent: **Apr. 16, 1996**

Apparatus for Remotely Altering & Monitoring
Brainwaves
Patent Number: **3,951,134**
Date of Patent: **Apr. 20, 1976**

Method & System for Altering Consciousness
Patent Number: **5,123,899**
Date of Patent: **Jun. 23, 1992**

Method of and Apparatus for Inducing Desired States
of Consciousness
Patent Number: **5,356,368**
Date of Patent: **Oct. 18, 1994**

Method & System for Brain Entrainment
Patent Number: **US 2014/0309484 A1**
Date of Patent: **Oct. 16, 2014**

Subliminal Acoustic Manipulation of Nervous Systems
In human subjects, sensory resonances can be excited
by subliminal atmospheric acoustic pulses that are
tuned to the resonance frequency. The 1/2 Hz sensory
resonance affects the autonomic nervous system and
may cause relaxation, drowsiness, or sexual
excitement, depending on the precise acoustic
frequency near 1/2 Hz used.
Patent Number: **6,017,302**
Date of Patent: **Jan. 25, 2000**

Method & Recording for Producing Sounds &
Messages To Achieve Alpha & Theta Brainwave States
& Positive Emotional States in Humans
Patent Number: **5,586,967**
Date of Patent: **Dec. 24, 1996**

FM Theta-Inducing Audible Sound, & Method, Device &
Recorded Medium To Generate the Same
Patent Number: **5,954,630**
Date of Patent: **Sep. 21, 1999**

Method, System & Apparatus for Remote Neural
Modulation Brain Stimulation and Feedback Control
Patent Number: **US 9.433,789 B2**
Date of Patent: **Sep. 6, 2016**

Laws

There are similar laws in each country.
Seek professional advice if necessary.

18 U.S. Code §☐241.
18 U.S. Code § 241 - Conspiracy against rights

18 U.S. Code §☐242.18
18 U.S. Code § 242 - Deprivation of rights
under color of law

U.S. Code §☐249.
18 U.S. Code § 249 - Hate crime acts

18 U.S. Code §☐875.
18 U.S. Code § 875 - Interstate
communications

18 U.S. Code §☐1111.
18 U.S. Code § 1111 - Murder

18 U.S. Code §☐1117.
18 U.S. Code § 1117 - Conspiracy to murder

18 U.S. Code §☐1512.
18 U.S. Code § 1512 - Tampering with a
witness, victim, or an informant

18 U.S. Code §☐1510.
18 U.S. Code § 1510 - Obstruction of criminal

investigations

18 U.S. Code § 1513.
18 U.S. Code § 1513 - Retaliating against a witness, victim, or an informant

18 U.S. Code § 1905.
18 U.S. Code § 1905 - Disclosure of confidential information generally

42 U.S. Code § 1983.
42 U.S. Code § 1983. Civil action for deprivation of rights

42 U.S. Code § 1985.
42 U.S. Code § 1985. Conspiracy to interfere with civil rights

18 U.S. Code § 2261A.
18 U.S. Code § 2261A - Stalking

18 U.S. Code § 2265.
18 U.S. Code § 2265 - Full faith and credit given to protection orders

18 U.S. Code § 2381.
18 U.S. Code § 2381 - Treason

18 U.S. Code § 2340A.
18 U.S. Code § 2340A - Torture

18 U.S. Code §☐2382.
18 U.S. Code § 2382 - Misprision of treason

18 U.S. Code §☐2389.
18 U.S. Code § 2389 - Recruiting for service against United States

31 U.S. Code §☐5328.
31 U.S. Code § 5328 - Whistleblower protections

47 U.S. Code §☐223.
47 U.S. Code § 223 - Obscene or harassing telephone calls in the District of Columbia or in interstate or foreign communications

18 U.S. Code CHAPTER 37
18 U.S. Code CHAPTER 37— ESPIONAGE AND CENSORSHIP

42 USC § 1985. Conspiracy to interfere with civil rights

21 U.S. Code §☐844. -----Substances / drugs / medications
21 U.S. Code § 844 - Penalties for simple possession

21 U.S. Code §☐841.
21 U.S. Code § 841 - Prohibited acts A

Court Cases

John St. Clair Akwei vs. NSA
Gangstalking : Court case - John St. Clair Awkei vs NSA

Gangstalking : Targeted Individual - Kathleen Watterson - Court Case - Short Summary

More court Cases :
Source:
http://www.justiceforallcitizens.com/electromagneti
cvictim.html

1) NORM RABIN'S COURT CASE
   UNITED STATES DISTRICT COURT/EASTERN DISTRICT OF NEW YORK -
   CASE NO: CV-93-3681, CASE NO: APPEAL NO: 936370, CASE NO: CV 984435
   Brief Synopsis - this case is regarding electromagnetic assaults, gang stalking, mind control, etc.

2) DAVID LARSON'S COURT CASE

UNITED STATES DISTRICT COURT/CENTRAL
DISTRICT OF CALIFORNIA - CASE NO: CV-09-01296
Brief Synopsis - this case is regarding implants and
residue left in his body from implants.

3) JAMES WALBERT'S COURT CASE
DISTRICT COURT OF SEDGWICK COUNTY,
KANSAS - CASE NO: 08-DM8647
Brief Synopsis - this case is regarding
electromagnetic assaults and gang stalking

4) JESUS MENDOZA COURT CASE-CASE NO: (S.D.
Tex) M03-38, U.S. S. CT. CASE NO: 04-9908,
U.S. COURT OF APPEAL FOR THE FIFTH
CIRCUIT CASE NO: 04-40095, CASE NO: 06-0155,
U.S. COURT OF APPEALS FOR THE DISTRICT OF
COLUMBIA CIRCUIT CASE NO: 06-5108
Brief Synopsis - this case is regarding
electromagnetic assaults and gang stalking, including
assaulting his children

5) CONNIE MARSHALL - U.S. COURT OF FEDERAL
CLAIMS CASE NO: 09-733C
Brief Synopsis - this case is regarding
electomagnetic assaults, gang stalking, destruction of
property (car engine
and radiator, washer, dryer, electric igniter switch on
heater in home, destruction of treadmill, computers, fax
machines, business and job, intercepting mail (even
registered and certified), attacking my pets, intercepting
email and
tele., changing my birth certificate, manipulating
social security records, increasing debt, constant
torture, torment and
harassment, etc. **NOTE: Ms. Marshall now has
several pending cases regarding related**

conspiracy in
that the Commonwealth of Kentucky is participating and creating the infrastructure to allow these crimes
to be committed against her. Ms. Marshall has signed certified receipts and/or taped the Officials on every
level in Kentucky stating, "We have been told not to assist you," and Danny Lawless, Police Officer stated,
"No one is going to assist you, because you are Redlined."

6) JOHN ST CLAIR AKWEI - CIVIL ACTION 92-0449
Brief Synopsis: This lawsuit reveals a frightening array of technologies and programs designed to keep tabs
on individuals.

7) STAN J. CATERBONE - U. S. DISTRICT COURT CASE NO: 05-2288

8) DONALD M. FRIEDMAN - CASE NO: 06-CV-2125
UNITED STATES DISTRICT COURT FOR THE DISTRICT OF COLUMBIA, FEDERAL DISTRICT
Brief Synopsis - this case is regarding directed energy and microwave weapons

9) JOHN FINCH - REF: OTP-CR-70/07 & EM_T01_OTP-CR-00122_07 & EM_Ack_OTP-CR-742_09
THE INTERNATIONAL CRIMINAL COURT (ICC)
Brief Synopsis - Electromagnetic Torture and Abuse

10)LAMBROS VS. FAULKNER, ET AL - CIVIL CASE

NO. 98-1621 (dsd/jmm)
UNITED STATES DISTRICT COURT OF MINNESOTA
Brief Synopsis: Torture, Forced Implantation and Transmitters in head. Swedish doctors familiar with treating
victims that have been implanted stated that foreign bodies do exist in Mr. Lambros and that they are most likely
transmitters. www.lambros.name/ricosuit4/rico24.html

11)GERAL W. SOSBEE - WRIT OF CERTIORARI NO. 01-182
SUPREME COURT OF THE UNITED STATES
Brief Synopsis: Electromagnetic Torture

12)BRIAN WRONGE - EASTERN DISTRICT COURT NO: (?)
Brief Synopsis: A doctor confirmed that he had metallice or paramagnetic foreign body in the region of the anterior
left axilla. An Anatonist stated: 'When I pass the microphone over his body it picks up vibration and white noise
sound waves that would be emitted by computer. When we had been doing this for a minute or so the sound dropped
as though someone had turned down the frequency somewhere. This happened in the area under his arm, near his
forehead and in some places along the vertebral column." It was also stated that these chips are probably operated by
some transmitter that the body sends sound waves out to.

13)THE INTERNATIONAL COMMITTEE ON MICROWAVE WEAPONS (ICOMW) -
HARLAN GIRARD
   U.S. DISTRICT COURT FOR THE DISTRICT OF COLUMBIA NO. (?)
   Brief Synopsis: Class Action Lawsuit regarding Offensive Microwave Weapons

14)JONES VS. AULT CITE 67 F.R.D. 124 (1974) CASE NO. CV474 - 279 *AND* CASE NO. 474 - 293
   U. S. DISTRICT COURT FOR THE SOUTH DISTRICT OF GEORGIA, SAVANNAH DISTRICT
   Brief Synopsis: Brain controlled and monitored by Electric or Parabolic Sound. Surveillance System tuned to brain
   wantonly monitors and combs body picking up sound and voices.

15)HUANG SI MING, HONG KONG PROFESSOR SUES THE U. S. FOR MIND CONTROL (FILED IN 1996)
   Brief Synopsis: Huang claims that one of the devices in his teeth can read his thoughts and talk to his mind while he
   is sleeping.

16)SOLEILMAVES, http://www.peacepink.ning.com
   Soleilmaves has filed several lawsuits regarding, "Remote Mind Control Abuses and Torture."
   A. International Criminal Court, Reference No. EM_T01_OTP-CR-00122_07
   B. United Nations Petitions Team - Results - No Reply, No Reference Number (Filed Lawsuit 2007)
   C. The Registrar European Court of Human Rights -

Counsel of Europe (Sent by Letter Dec. 2009)
. Results: No Reply Yet, No Case Number
D. Curia - To: The Registry - Rue Du Fort
Niedergrunewald - L-2925 Luxembourg (Sent by Letter
Dec. 2009)
Case Ref: No: T-507109AJ

17)JAMES GEE - REFERENCE NO: EM_ACK_OTP-
CR-742_09
INTERNATIONAL CRIMINAL COURT
Head of the Information and Evidence Unit - Office of
the Prosecutor - P.O. Box 19519
2500 CM the Hague, The Netherlands

****
**Type the following in your web browser to see the
first
Los Angeles Billboard regarding Electronic
Harassment and Stalking**

http://www.multistalkervictims.org/labillboardjan31
11.jpg
****

More cases here:
http://peacepink.ning.com/forum/topics/lawsuits-of-
mind-control

Source:
**http://www.justiceforallcitizens.com/electromagneti
cvictim.html**

Resources For targeted Individuals

Do - Do Not And Tips

Do:

- Gather evidence: Pictures, call recordings, voice recordings, text messages, emails, mails, screen shoots...etc
- Keep multiple copies of your evidence, online and offline.
- Inform people about Gang Stalking
- Inform people about the mind control technology
- Inform people about the fake Ti's
- Print Flyers and hand them in your community, workplace...etc
- On social media block everyone who's harassing you
- Connect with real Ti's
- Share resources and solutions
- Download good YouYube videos on your computer
- If you find a good website, copy and paste the content in a text file on your computer.

Do Not:
- Do not donate money to any 'organization'
- Do not buy any devices sold as solutions for Ti's
- Do not stay quiet
- Do not believe everything you read online
- Do not seek Psychiatric help/advice
- Do not overreact
- Do not trust the police, many are involved, and the rest don't care
- Do not give up hope
- Do not do as they say
- Do not commit suicide

Tips:
- Many fake Ti's = Perps(Gang Stalkers)
- Many Facebook groups run by perps
- Many videos on youtube are made by perps
- Many books are written by perps
- Many websites made by perps
- Always record and documents your experiences
- Be careful whom you trust
- Beat them at their own game, remembers, this is an action-reaction psychological war
- They want you angry - stay calm
- They want you agitated - stay calm
- They want you jobless - get a job
- They want you upset - be happy
- They want you to kill somebody - show them mercy
- They want you to seek psychiatric help - stay away from psychiatrists

-Do not tell anyone that you are a Targeted Individual, gather evidence first. In the main time, inform people about the Gangstalking program and the mind control technologies.

- Once you have enough evidence, and you can explain it, you are safe to tell anyone that you are a Targeted Individual. Evidence can only be ridiculed and ignored, not denied.

-How to identify a gangstalker ?

They are the "spectators", they pay the people that come into contact with you to harass you, and they stay close by and watch "the show", always look around for those who pay attention to what's going on with you, those paying attention are the real perps, if you have a camera, make sure you record them.

- Not all so-called gangstalkers are gangstalkers, many are random people that come into contact with the Ti.
Not all the people recruited to harass(pass a message) know that they are taking part in a psychological operation, and other teens or hundreds or of people before them have passed the same message.
Also, people aren't told that the Ti might snap and hurt or even kill them.
That's why we, the Targeted Individuals, need to educate the general public about Gangstalking.

-Manipulation of Information
Those who are aware of the gang stalker's technology, tactics, and techniques, are very difficult to be manipulated.
Those who are not aware, fall for this trick, and other cheap tricks.
Let's say for example your mom is using Facebook a lot, gang stalkers will make posts, articles, videos, and other stuff related to what

you're thinking/doing and show it to her on her Facebook.

Now, when she meets you she will start talking to you about those things she saw on Facebook.

Gangstalkers will do the same thing with the TV, radio, newspapers, or whatever the person close to you, is into. They did that to my mom, so basically, my mom had a normal conversation with me, while she was "harassing me" without knowing it.

If that makes sense...

-Threatening to harm or kill your family members.

Gang stalkers often threaten to kill the Ti's family members if the Ti's does not obey and do as they say.

Gather evidence on the threats and warn your family members of the threats, advise them to be cautious and attentive to any changes in their surroundings.

Blindly following the Gangstalkers orders should not be an option.

With this threat sometimes comes the "suicide" order.

"If you do not kill yourself, we will kill your kid, mother, father, brother"

DO NOT COMMIT SUICIDE.

Important - Evidence - Examples How-To
- You can gather evidence online and offline.

The anchors and triggers will be your evidence

The triggers are part of a behavior modification program called NLP (neuro-linguistic programming) which uses **anchors and triggers** to promote change. An **anchor** is created when an emotional state is linked to something such as an object, person, sound, smell, place, color, etc. Once the **anchor** is established, whatever the individual was exposed to during the **anchoring** process becomes the stimulus (**trigger**) that will provoke the emotion. So basically, PO is simply a series of "stimulus-response" interactions.

Write down the anchoring words, numbers, colors, phrases, objects,etc.
Document everything, online (*social media memes, messages, emails, texts, calls*) and offline (*home, work, shopping, barber, doctor,etc*)
Mix and match your online and offline records.

Remember:
This is done **repeatedly(Sensitisation-Anchoring-Triggers)**, it has to be done repeatedly, otherwise, the whole program would be useless. **Repetition** is what makes it easy to be explained and proven.

Please watch the videos below to see few very important examples.

Gang stalking : ABC News Couple Harassed with Organized Gang Stalking Noise Harassment Campaign

GangStalking, Targeted individuals, Cyber Harassment, Cyber stalking, Cyber Torture, Sensitization

Gang stalking - Cyber Stalking and Harassment - Targeted Individuals - Cyber Torture

Police Gang stalking operations and tactics

Other Recommended Videos

The Gangstalking Program Explained
https://odysee.com/@GangStalking-Aattention-Awareness:8/the-gangstalking-program-explained:4

Bright Light on Black Shadows, Chapter18-Dr.Rauni Kilde- Gang stalkers TRAINING MANUAL Gang stalking
https://odysee.com/@GangStalking-Aattention-Awareness:8/bright-light-on-black-shadows,-chapter18:b

Gang Stalking : DEW, Sonic, Low Frequency Weapons - Mind Control Behavior Control - PATENTS REVIEW
https://odysee.com/@GangStalking-Aattention-Awareness:8/gang-stalking-dew-sonic-low-frequency:2

Gang Stalking Technology - Everything YOU NEED TO KNOW !?!
https://odysee.com/@GangStalking-Aattention-Awareness:8/gang-stalking-technology-everything-you:c

Schizophrenia Or Not
https://odysee.com/@GangStalking-Aattention-Awareness:8/schizophrenia-or-not:1

Gang stalking - Darpa Avatar Project Links Your Mind To A Digital World Inside A Quantum Computer

https://odysee.com/gang-stalking-darpa-avatar-project-links:302d9c52ab10dca27427fc13d6a001163263c99f

GangStalking, Understanding Organized Gangstalking and Electronic Harassment, Cyber Torture

https://odysee.com/gangstalking,-understanding-organized:7ec0e8bbdf2cabbdf33a676f1249b8fb605e1981

Stephen Shellen Targeted Individual, Gang stalking, Cyber Torture,Mind Control,Electronic Harassment

https://odysee.com/stephen-shellen-targeted-individual-gang:2a0075e08640415ce7559a95deb546777ddeb03f

GangStalking: Phone Spoofing and Voice Transformation /cloning - Targeted Individuals - CyberTorture

https://odysee.com/@GangStalking-Aattention-Awareness:8/gangstalking-phone-spoofing-and-voice:4

Gangstalking : Court case - John St. Clair Awkei vs NSA

https://odysee.com/@GangStalking-Aattention-Awareness:8/gangstalking-court-case-john-st-clair:9

Gangstalking : Targeted Individual - Kathleen Watterson - Court Case - Short Summary

WhisleBlowers

* Dr. Barrie Trower - MI6
* Willam Binney - NSA
* Kirk Weibe - NSA
* Carl Clark - Ex mossad / CIA
* Carl Clark - CIA
* Kevin Shipp - CIA
* Mark Phillips - CIA
* John DeCamp - Army
* Brian Tew D.O.D

* **Bryan Kofron aka Justin Carter** - Former SIS(Security Industries Specialists, Inc.) He identifies the following "Private Security" contracting companies as being deeply involved in "the Program:" Amazon, Blackwater, Academi, Pinkerton's National Detective Agency, G4S, Dyncorp Security-Protection, Security Industries Specialists, Inc. (SIS), Scientific Applications International Corporation (SAIC), Infragard, and Lockheed Martin.

Dr Eric Karlstrom - Profesor of geography , California State University, Stanislaus
https://gangstalkingmindcontrolcults.com/

Dr. John Hall - Anesthesiologist living in San Antonio, Texas

Books:
- A New Breed Satellite Terrorism
- Guinea Pigs: Technologies of Control

Dr. Nick Begich is the eldest son of the late United States Congressman from Alaska, Nick Begich Sr., and political activist Pegge Begich
Book: Controlling the Human Mind - The Technologies of Political Control or Tools for Peak Performance.

Dr. Robert Duncan - Ex-CIA Mind Control Scientist And Author
Books:
- Project: Soul Catcher: Secrets of Cyber and Cybernetic Warfare Revealed
- How to Tame a Demon: A short practical guide to organized intimidation stalking, electronic torture, and mind control
- The matrix deciphered

Dr. Ben Colodzin - Psychologist
Books:
- The CIA Doctors: Human Rights Violations By American Psychiatrists
- Military Mind Control: A Story of Trauma and Recovery
- The Great Psychiatry Scam.

Dr Paul Marko
- Assasinated By CIA S.A.T.A.N. Systemn

Days After Eemailing Whisle Blower Bryan Tew
https://pineconeutopia.wordpress.com/

Curtis Bennett - Adjunct Professor
Curtis has a background in electrical energy provision and building engineering, and as a journeyman electrician. He has worked as a thermal radiation consultant and an Adjunct Professor, lecturing for accredited continuing medical education credits internationally.

Dr. Sean Andrews Ph.D., Materials Science
M.S., Organic Chemistry
Dr. Harold Mandel–The Tyranny of Psychiatry
Dr. Terry Robertson
Dr. Michael Hoffer
And many more...

Recommended Books

* Dr. John Hall
- A New Breed Satellite Terrorism
- Guinea Pigs: Technologies of Control

* Dr. Robert Duncan
- Project: Soul Catcher: Secrets of Cyber and Cybernetic Warfare Revealed
- How to Tame a Demon: A short practical guide to organized intimidation stalking, electronic torture, and mind control
- The matrix deciphered

* Dr. Ben Colodzin
- The CIA Doctors: Human Rights Violations By American Psychiatrists
- Military Mind Control: A Story of Trauma and Recovery
- The Great Psychiatry Scam.

* Rauni Kilde
- Bright Light On Dark Shadows

* Albert Pike - MORALS and DOGMA

* Thomas E. Bearden
- Star Wars Now :The Bohm Aharonov Effect, Scalar Interferometry, and   Soviet Weaponization

* **Steven Hassan**
- Combatting Cult Mind Control

* **Gordon Corera**
-Cyberspies

* **V.N. Binhi**
- Electromagnetic Mind Control

* **Walter Bowart**
- OPERATION MIND CONTROL

* **Sergei A. Vakin - Lev N. Shustov - Robert H. Dunwell**
- Fundamentals of Electronic Warfare

* **Max More and Natasha Vita-More**
- The Transhumanist Reader

* **Julie K. Petersen**
- Understanding Surveillance

* **John D. Marks**
- The Search for the "Manchurian Candidate *(1979)*

Klaus behnke / Jurgen Fuchs (Hg)
- Zersetzung Der Seele (Decomposition of the Soul)

* Trevor Aaronson
- The Terror Factory: Inside the FBI's Manufactured War on Terror

Recommended Websites

www.gangstalkingmindcontrolcults.com/

www.peacepink.ning.com/

www.greatdreams.com/RNM.htm

www.mindpowernews.com/ESPOfEspionage.htm

https://www.targetedjustice.com/

www.freedomfortargetedindividuals.org

www.surveillancesurvivors.org/

www.rexresearch.com/sublimin/sublimin.htm

www.mikrowellenterror.de/

www.ewaffen.blogsport.de

https://www.targetedindividualscanada.com

www.mindjustice.org/

https://projectsvoice.weebly.com/

www.sosbeevfbi.com

Facebook Groups

GangStalking AattentionAwareness
GangStalking Romania
Grupo de Targeted Individuals Argentina
Targeted Individuals in Canada
Targeted Individuals - Malaysia
Brazil TIs
Targeted Individuals Panama
Targeted Individuals Chile
Targeted Individuals Latam
Targeted Individuals Mexica
Targeted Individuals Ecuador
Targeted Individuals Belgium and Holland
Individus Cibles / Targeted Individuals France
William Binney and Kirk Wiebe Support
Targeted Individuals TI
Targeted Individuals in Germany
Gang stalking in Deutschland - opfer berichten
South Korea voice to skull victims
Targeted Individuals / Mk Ultra Canada &
World
Mind Control France
Targeted Individuals - New Zeeland

Youtube Channels

GangStalking Aattention Awareness

Steve News - www.stephenshellenberger.com/
Erik Karlstrom
Ramola D Reports
A Simulated Reality
GangStalking Survival
Shad Budge Productions
Ella FFTI
Autumn Targeted Individual in NZ
Targeted Lives Matter
Organized GangStalking
Targeted Individuals
Gangstalking Fight Back

There are many more, **some** are created by the gang stalkers.
Gang stalkers make videos overreacting, talking a lot about nonsensical stuff, looking paranoid, pointing in the wrong directions, and seeking a lot of attention.
All this is design to discredit the real Ti's and make the rest look crazy.
Those overreacting or sounding crazy are Gang stalkers and should be labeled as such.

Contact

Facebook Group: Gangstalking AattentionAwareness

Facebook Page: Gangstalking Aattention Awareness

Youtube Channel: Gangstalking Aattention Awareness

LBRY: Gangstalking Aattention Awareness

Donation Link:

Bonus

Free PDF version of this book.

1- Free PDF version - read it on any device
2- Check the authenticity of this book

Click the link below ;-) Nope, you won't :-)
Type the link below in any browser:
https://drive.google.com/file/d/1gwk-
MQJYMQdFcGxVl_bkNhLMDExmEu6w/view?
usp=sharing

_OR_

Scan the QR Code with your mobile phone

What is Gangstalking?

Gangstalking is a form of community mobbing and organised stalking combined. Just like you have workplace mobbing, and online mobbing, which are both fully recognised as legitimate, this is also the community form, plus electronic arassment.

Find out more:

Fb G: Gangstalking AattentionAwareness
Fb P: Gangstalking Aattention Awareness
LBRY: Gangstalking Aattention Awareness
YT: Gangstalking Aattention Awareness
Inst: gs_aattention_awareness

Game over

⊘Let's stop this thieves and murderers⊘

The End

Is Near

To Be Continued...

Made in the USA
Coppell, TX
06 December 2024

41857404R10079